IRE

101 Quick Questions
with Catholic Answers

Marriage, Divorce, and Annulment

101 Quick Questions with Catholic Answers

Marriage, Divorce, and Annulment

Jim Blackburn

San Diego
2011

Published by Catholic Answers
2020 Gillespie Way
El Cajon, California 92020

619-387-7200

www.catholic.com

Cover by Devin Schadt
Interior design by Russell Design

Printed in the United States of America

ISBN 978-1-933919-42-3

3340059

TABLE OF CONTENTS

Introduction

Index

INTRODUCTION

Human beings have a history of botching it when it comes to marriage, so it should come as no surprise that the Church has found it necessary to devote so much of its law to it. The Old Testament is filled with examples of concubinage, adultery, divorce, serial marriages, and polygamy—and that's among God's chosen people. But Jesus expects his followers to get it right when it comes to marriage, the way God originally intended it (cf. Mk 10:1-12).

The Catholic Church takes this seriously and so has instituted laws governing marriage for Catholics. The Church has the authority to teach and make laws about marriage because Jesus gave it. He said, first to Peter and later to the all the apostles, "Whatever you bind on earth shall be bound in heaven, and whatever you loose on earth shall be loosed in heaven" (Mt 16:19; 18:18). With these words he gave our first pope and first Church hierarchy, among other things, the authority to enact laws which the faithful are obliged to observe:

> The power to "bind and loose" connotes the authority to absolve sins, to pronounce doctrinal judgments, and to make disciplinary decisions in the Church. Jesus entrusted this authority to the Church through the ministry of the apostles and in particular through the ministry of Peter, the only one to whom he specifically entrusted the keys of the kingdom. (*Catechism of the Catholic Church,* 553)

Today, the Church's *Code of Canon Law* contains 111

individual canons governing marriage. This may sound like a lot, but compared to the number of marriage laws civil governments impose on their citizens it is not. Even so, these canons represent more than six percent of the 1,752 canons contained in the *Code*.

These laws are there for our benefit, to help us treat the institution of marriage and the sacrament of matrimony with the dignity and respect it deserves. But while these laws are helpful, they often can be misunderstood or difficult to follow. Not a few Catholics today find themselves facing marriage-related situations they're not sure how to deal with in a way that conforms to Church teaching and law.

May I attend this wedding? Can I marry this person? Is my marriage valid? Can I get a divorce? May I still receive Communion? Do I need an annulment? What about remarriage? The list of questions seems endless. Indeed, marriage-related questions are one of the most common topics dealt with by Catholic apologists.

In this volume, I have compiled 100 questions representative of the spectrum of marriage-related questions the Catholic Answers apologists, including myself, have answered over the years. I hope these questions and answers will help you to more fully understand the Catholic Church's teaching and laws concerning marriage so that you can be assured of always treating marriage with the dignity and respect that God originally intended for this sacred institution.

—Jim Blackburn

ABBREVIATIONS

CCC – *Catechism of the Catholic Church*
CIC – *Code of Canon Law*
RSV – Revised Standard Version

Weddings/
Who Can Wed

Q: Why can't Catholics get married outdoors? We want to get married outdoors where God made everything, and we can be surrounded by his creation.

A: Customs differ widely between cultures regarding the place of celebration for marriage. In Western culture, weddings traditionally take place in a church to symbolize the sacred nature of the act being performed. Thus the *Code of Canon Law* specifies that:

§1. Marriage between Catholics or between a Catholic and a baptized non-Catholic party is to be celebrated in a parish church; with the permission of the local ordinary or the pastor, it can be celebrated in another church or oratory.

§2. The local ordinary can permit marriage to be celebrated in some other suitable place.

§3. Marriage between a Catholic party and a non-baptized party can be celebrated in a church or in some other suitable place. (CIC 1118)

Note that a distinction is drawn between the marriage of baptized individuals (§§ 1-2) and marriage between a baptized and non-baptized party (§3). This suggests that the stronger requirement for celebration in a church in the former case is intended to emphasize the sacramental character of the marriage, since the former marriage is sacramental while the latter is not.

It is also generally the case that a Catholic marriage is celebrated in the context of a Mass, and the Mass must normally be celebrated in a sacred (i.e., consecrated) place (CIC 932 §1). Out-of-doors doesn't count.

Q: My fiancé and I would like to have a medieval-themed wedding and nuptial Mass, but our parents are disappointed with our plans and complain that a theme is inappropriate for a Catholic wedding. Is this true?

A: Your parents may fear that your chosen theme will undermine the sense of the sacredness of the event. This is a particularly valid concern when it comes to the Mass itself, where the focus needs to be clearly on the sacraments rather than on any theme. The reception, on the other hand, is an appropriate place for individual expression. In making your plans, keep in mind that you want your guests to notice more that it was a Catholic wedding than that it was a theme wedding.

Q: Is it true that the wedding march song cannot be played during a Catholic wedding?

A: Many Catholic parishes recommend that "The Bridal Chorus" from Richard Wagner's opera *Lohengrin* not be used because it is secular music. Ideally, only liturgical music should be used during a Catholic wedding. However, some parishes are more lenient on the issue than others and will allow secular classical music. A prospective couple should check with the wedding coordinator of the parish where they are to marry to determine local protocol.

Q: I heard that a bishop allowed a nun to marry a couple. Does the bishop have the authority to do this?

A: The *Code of Canon Law* makes provision when certain conditions exist for lay persons, including nuns, to assist at weddings:

> Where there is a lack of priests and deacons, the diocesan bishop can delegate lay persons to assist at marriages, with the previous favorable vote of the conference of bishops and after he has obtained the permission of the Holy See. (CIC 1112)

Q: Can a practicing Catholic officiate at a civil wedding ceremony?

A: Yes, a Catholic could preside at a civil wedding ceremony under some circumstances:

1. The couple must be non-Catholics not bound by Catholic marital law.
2. There must be no obvious impediments to their marriage (e.g., previous marriage, close blood relationship).
3. The Catholic must be authorized by the state to officiate at civil wedding ceremonies (e.g., judge, justice of the peace, other recognized official).

A Catholic cannot obtain "ordination" from a mail-order or online "ordination" mill, even if his state recognizes marriages performed by individuals who have obtained such "ordinations."

Q: The Universal Life church offers quick, free ordinations online that allow someone to officiate at a civil wedding. Can a Catholic obtain such an ordination?

A: There are two principles to keep in mind here: First, a Catholic cannot accept "ordination" in a non-Catholic church because such "ordination" is invalid and because it gives the appearance that one has joined and ministers in a non-Catholic church. Second, assuming that there are no obvious impediments to marriage, a lay Catholic who is qualified by the state to preside at civil marriages may do so for non-Catholics who are not bound by Catholic marital law.

In short, although a Catholic may not try to become "ordained" in a non-Catholic church in order to officiate at a civil wedding, if he is qualified by the state by some other licit means to preside at civil weddings (e.g., judge, justice of the peace), he can preside at a civil wedding under the conditions mentioned above.

Q: At our wedding rehearsal, the priest told me that during Communion he would give me the chalice with the precious blood. After I received, I was to give the chalice to my wife and say "The blood of Christ, my wife." Did I do something wrong?

A: Your priest was wrong on two counts. First, while a priest can depute an individual person to administer Holy Communion on a particular occasion, there must be a necessity that requires this, such as having more communicants than the priest himself can minister to. He thus should not have asked you to give the chalice to your wife alone. Secondly, the formula with which Communion is distributed does not include "my wife." According to paragraphs 41 and 43 of the *Norms for the Distribution and Reception of Holy Communion* (available from usccb.org), a minister of Communion says "The body of Christ" or "The blood of Christ" and does not add anything else.

Because you were acting on your priest's instructions and, at the time, had no reason to believe that he was incorrect, you are not culpable for wrongdoing by giving your wife Communion. The one who bears responsibility is the priest, who should have been aware of the norms of the distribution of Communion.

Q: Can a non-Catholic Christian groom receive Communion at his Catholic wedding?

A: No, the non-Catholic may not receive Communion at a Catholic wedding. Actually, not all Catholics may receive Communion. Only those who are in a state of grace can receive the Eucharist. To receive Communion in the Catholic Church is a sign of complete acceptance of Catholic teaching. It is also a sign of complete unity among believers. Unfortunately, Catholic and non-Catholic Christians still do not share such unity. At present, the mutual reception of Communion by Catholics and non-Catholics would not be an honest sign. Because of the inability of non-Catholic Christians to receive Communion, Catholics who are marrying a non-Catholic are usually encouraged not to have a Mass as part of their nuptial liturgy.

Q: Are there any circumstances that would allow a Catholic to receive communion at a Lutheran wedding? Would it be better to receive, knowing that this not the body and blood of Christ, if everyone else does?

A: No. There are limited circumstances in which it is permissible for Catholics to receive Communion from non-Catholic ministers. These conditions are set forth in the *Code of Canon Law*:

> Whenever necessity requires or genuine spiritual advantage suggests, and provided that the danger of error or indifferentism is avoided, it is lawful for the faithful for whom it is physically or morally impossible to approach a Catholic minister, to receive the sacraments of penance, Eucharist, and anointing of the sick from non-Catholic ministers in whose churches these sacraments are valid. (CIC 844:2)

Lutherans do not have a validly ordained ministerial priesthood and so do not have a valid Eucharist. The fact that other people are participating in the Lutheran communion does not change one's obligation under this canon.

The need to be faithful in this matter is particularly underscored in another part of the *Code*: "The Christian faithful are bound by an obligation, even in their own patterns of activity, always to maintain communion with the Church" (CIC 209:1).

Q: If a Lutheran couple asked a Catholic friend to read a Scripture passage at their Lutheran wedding service, could the Catholic friend do so?

A: Regarding Catholics participating in readings at non-Catholic churches, the Vatican document *Directory for the Application of Principles and Norms on Ecumenism* says this: "In liturgical celebrations taking place in other churches and ecclesial communities, Catholics are encouraged to take part in the psalms, responses, hymns, and common actions of the church in which they are guests. If invited by their hosts, they may read a lesson or preach" (PNE 118).

Q: My daughter and her fiancé recently left the Catholic Church for a nondenominational one. They will be marrying soon in the same church and have asked me to participate in lighting the unity candle as a symbol of their marital union. Is it acceptable for me to do so?

A: I recommend you decline. As former Catholics, your daughter and her fiancé almost certainly still are bound to observe the Catholic form of marriage, and their marriage in the non-Catholic church will be invalid. While there is no official Church teaching on this issue, lighting the unity candle with your daughter would send the wrong message: 1) tacit approval of a marriage not recognized by the Church, and 2) great potential to cause scandal.

The *Catechism of the Catholic Church* defines scandal as "an attitude or behavior which leads another to do evil. The person who gives scandal becomes his neighbor's tempter. He damages virtue and integrity; he may even draw his brother into spiritual death. Scandal is a grave offense if by deed or omission another is deliberately led into a grave offense" (CCC 2284).

Q: I was a groomsman in a Methodist wedding this weekend. This experience raised a few questions. (1) Does the Catholic Church consider Protestant marriages valid? (2) The minister or presider was a woman; since the priesthood is reserved for men, does this make things worse? (3) At the reception, I was invited to another wedding in which the presider will be the groom's father, who's not even an active preacher; would this marriage be valid? (4) Lastly, did I do anything wrong by participating in the wedding?

A: Protestants are not under the same canonical requirements as Catholics to be married in the Church by a priest or deacon. Since they are baptized, the Catholic Church considers their marriages to be valid and sacramental, even though their own theology doesn't consider marriage a sacrament. In a Catholic wedding, the minister is required as an official witness of the Church, but for non-Catholics the validity of the marriage is not affected by whether the officiant is a man or woman or a minister or a justice of the peace.

Assuming that both the bride and the groom were Protestant and were otherwise free to marry, it was not wrong for you to participate in this wedding as an official witness, although if you thought it might be wrong, you ought to have found out before the wedding. (Now that you know, you can feel free to accept the invitation to that second wedding, again assuming that both spouses-to-be are Protestant.)

Q: If I were to marry a Lutheran, could both a Catholic priest and a Lutheran pastor have roles in the service?

A: It is possible to have both ministers involved in the ceremony in some capacity.

The 1993 *Directory on Ecumenism* states:

> With the previous authorization of the local ordinary, and if invited to do so, a Catholic priest or deacon may attend or participate in some way in the celebration of mixed marriages, in situations where the dispensation from canonical form has been granted. In these cases, there may be only one ceremony in which the presiding person receives the marriage vows. At the invitation of this celebrant, the Catholic priest or deacon may offer other appropriate prayers, read from the Scriptures, give a brief exhortation, and bless the couple.
>
> Upon request of the couple, the local ordinary may permit the Catholic priest to invite the minister of the party of the other church or ecclesial community to participate in the celebration of the marriage, to read from the Scriptures, give a brief exhortation and bless the couple.
>
> Because of problems concerning eucharistic sharing which may arise from the presence of non-Catholic witnesses and guests, a mixed marriage celebrated according to the Catholic form ordinarily takes place outside the eucharistic liturgy. (157–159)

Q: A Catholic couple is getting married in the Episcopal church by Episcopal clergy. Both bride and groom are Catholics and wanted to marry in the Catholic Church, but the bride is divorced, and the annulment has not been completed yet. They have chosen to get married now in the Episcopal church and then later marry in the Catholic Church. As a Catholic, attending the ceremony seems improper to me.

A: You are correct. To enter into an invalid marriage for reasons of convenience is sinful and betrays a lack of good judgment. It can also give scandal to those who are not knowledgeable in their Catholic faith.

Q: My Catholic friend is engaged to a divorced man, and they are awaiting his annulment. They were told that it was okay to get married by a justice of the peace and then, when his annulment comes through, have their marriage blessed in the Church. Is this really okay?

A: No, this is definitely not okay. A Catholic cannot validly marry outside the Church without permission (cf. *Code of Canon Law* 1108), so a civil ceremony and subsequent Church blessing is not a moral option. The Church presumes the first marriage to be valid unless and until proven otherwise through the annulment process, so your friend should not even be dating him.

Consider this scenario: The couple marries civilly and then the Church's marriage tribunal finds his first marriage to be valid—he doesn't get the annulment. Your friend will be civilly married to a man whom the Church recognizes is already married to someone else. She'll actually be living and sleeping with another woman's husband. She won't be able to have her marriage blessed in the Church. And, as long as she continues to live as though she's married to this man, she'll be barred from receiving the Eucharist and won't be able to receive absolution through the sacrament of penance. What a mess!

Your friend needs to take a step back and wait for the results of the annulment process. Only then will she know whether this relationship is something she can morally pursue.

Q: Are prenuptial agreements forbidden?

A: Although canon law does not mention the topic of prenuptial agreements, the Catholic Church teaches that marriage is the complete giving of the spouses to God through
each other. Therefore, there can be no strings attached. A
prenuptial agreement is a very big string!

Q: Is it OK for Catholics to have their marriage witnessed by a priest of the Society of St. Pius X?

A: According to the *Code of Canon Law*, Catholic marriages ordinarily must be witnessed by the local ordinary or the parish priest, or by a minister—usually a priest or deacon—delegated by them to do so (1108 §1). Because SSPX priests do not have faculties from the Church to witness Catholic marriages, Catholics may not have their marriage witnessed by an SSPX priest.

Q: My cousin (who has been baptized and confirmed in the Catholic Church) and her fiancé (who has been baptized Catholic) plan to get married by a priest of an "independent catholic church." Will this be a valid, sacramental marriage? Will they excommunicate themselves?

A: Since both are Catholics, your cousin and her fiancé are bound by Church law to marry in the Church. The *Code of Canon Law* establishes the form of the celebration of marriage which generally "must be observed if at least one of the parties contracting marriage was baptized in the Catholic Church or received into it and has not defected from it by a formal act" (CIC 1117). Marrying in an "independent catholic church" will not satisfy this obligation and the resulting "marriage" will be invalid.

Although they will not incur excommunication for this, a conjugal relationship outside a valid marriage is grave matter and they should not receive the Eucharist until the matter is rectified and they have been to confession. You would do well to express your concerns and strongly encourage them to marry validly in the Church.

Q: Does a baptized Catholic who has received first confession and First Communion need to be confirmed to be married in the Catholic Church?

A: While it is not an absolute requirement that Catholics be confirmed before they are married in the Church, confirmation before marriage is something the Church strongly urges. The *Code of Canon Law* states: "Catholics who have not yet received the sacrament of confirmation are to receive it before being admitted to marriage, if this can be done without grave inconvenience" (CIC 1065).

Q: Are racially mixed marriages permissible, or do we have an obligation to keep the races distinct?

A: Mixed-race marriages are permissible. This is indicated by biblical example in both the Old and the New Testaments. In the Old Testament, Joseph's wife was the daughter of an Egyptian high priest (Gn 41:45), and he had two sons by her (41:50-52), who were then adopted by his father Jacob (48:5-6) and became the progenitors of the tribes of Ephraim and Manasseh, even though they were half-Egyptian.

Moses also married the daughter of a foreign priest (Ex 2:21, 3:1), and the fact he had taken a foreign wife became a bone of contention with his brother and sister (Nm 12:1), but God vindicated him of this and other charges (Nm 12:8).

In the New Testament, Timothy was the product of an ethnically mixed marriage since he had a mother who was a Jew but a father who was a Greek (Acts 16:1).

Because interracial marriages are not condemned anywhere in Scripture, because the biblical example includes interracial marriages, and because Christ, in one sense, has obliterated all ethnic divisions (Col 3:11) and rendered all people clean so there is no need for ethnic separation (Acts 10:28-29, Gal 2:11-14), interracial marriages are permissible.

Q: Is marrying a relative allowed by the Church?

A: Consanguinity in the direct line (e.g., father-daughter, grandmother-grandson) always prohibits marriage. In the indirect line, those related only as closely as first cousins are impeded from marrying (CIC 1091), but such an impediment for first cousins may be dispensed by the bishop.

Q: Why did England's King Henry VIII, who had never been married, need a dispensation from Rome to marry his brother's widow, Catherine of Aragon? Would the Church prohibit such a marriage today?

A: Henry VIII (r. 1509-1547) was granted a dispensation from the impediment of affinity. Today, the impediment of affinity arises between a person and his or her spouse's direct-line relatives. For example, a widower is impeded from marrying his deceased wife's mother, grandmother, daughter, granddaughter, etc. (CIC 1092).

In the 16th century, though, the impediment of affinity came about merely through intercourse (marriage was not required) and extended further than the direct line of relatives. Since it was presumed that Catherine of Aragon had intercourse with her husband, Henry's brother, the impediment of affinity had to be dispensed before Catherine and Henry could validly marry.

Q: If a person is infertile through no fault of his own, can he get married in the Catholic Church?

A: You may be confusing infertility with impotence. Infertility (the inability to procreate children) is not an impediment to marriage; permanent and irreversible impotence (the inability to consummate a marriage through marital relations) is an impediment. Impotence that is known at the time of the marriage to be permanent and irreversible is a barrier to marriage, because the couple must be capable of consummating their marriage. If the couple has reason to assume that the impotence can be treated or reversed, they may get married.

Q: If you get married in Jamaica, can you come back to the States and have your marriage blessed by the Catholic Church?

A: Getting married in Jamaica is not an impediment to a valid marriage, and those who validly marry there are not required to travel to the United States in order to have their marriage blessed, or convalidated.

Catholics are required to be married in the Church; if one marries outside the Church, whether in or out of the United States, then one's marriage will not be valid unless it is later convalidated. To marry deliberately outside of the Church and live as husband and wife is not a minor irregularity that one can plan to straighten out later; it is a grave betrayal of our obligation as Catholics to live by the law of the Church and a sin against God, in whose eyes the marriage is nonexistent.

Mixed
Marriages

Q: Can a priest, as a matter of personal conscience, refuse to marry a Catholic with a non-Catholic?

A: The Catholic Church does give dispensations for Catholics to marry members of other Christian churches or other religions. A priest may refuse to witness a marriage because he judges one or both parties to be too young or lacking in sufficient psychological maturity, etc. Further, the priest may refuse to officiate, but he cannot prevent the couple from going to another priest who might have a different pastoral opinion. All things being equal, Catholics have a right to the sacraments.

Q: If a baptized Catholic marries a non-baptized person, is that a valid marriage? Are there any special requirements?

A: The *Code of Canon Law* allows this by dispensation only. Here are the requirements for dispensation:

> The local ordinary can grant a permission of this kind if there is a just and reasonable cause. He is not to grant it unless the following conditions have been fulfilled:
>
> [T]he Catholic party is to declare that he or she is prepared to remove dangers of defecting from the faith and is to make a sincere promise to do all in his or her power so that all offspring are baptized and brought up in the Catholic Church; the other party is to be informed at an appropriate time about the promises which the Catholic party is to make, in such a way that it is certain that he or she is truly aware of the promise and obligation of the Catholic party; both parties are to be instructed about the purposes and essential properties of marriage which neither of the contracting parties is to exclude. (CIC 1125)

Q: Is a Catholic allowed to marry a non-Christian?

A: The Catholic Church calls this situation "disparity of cult," and there are circumstances in which it may be allowed. Here is what the *Catechism of the Catholic Church* teaches about disparity of cult and mixed marriage (marriage between a Catholic and a baptized non-Catholic):

> Difference of confession between the spouses does not constitute an insurmountable obstacle for marriage ... But the difficulties of mixed marriages must not be underestimated ... The spouses risk experiencing the tragedy of Christian disunity even in the heart of their own home. Disparity of cult can further aggravate these difficulties. Differences about faith and the very notion of marriage, but also different religious mentalities, can become sources of tension in marriage, especially as regards the education of children. The temptation to religious indifference can then arise.
>
> ... [A] mixed marriage needs for liceity the express permission of ecclesiastical authority. In case of disparity of cult an express dispensation from this impediment is required for the validity of the marriage. This permission or dispensation presupposes that both parties know and do not exclude the essential ends and properties of marriage; and furthermore that the Catholic party confirms the obligations, which have been made known to the non-Catholic party, of preserving his or her own faith and ensuring the baptism and education of the children in the Catholic Church. (CCC 1634-1635)

Q: When my wife and I were married in the Catholic Church, I was a baptized Catholic and she was a non-practicing Jehovah's Witness. At that time she was not baptized, but she has since been baptized in the Catholic Church. Is our marriage a sacramental marriage?

A: Yes, your marriage is sacramental. There are two requirements for a marriage to be sacramental: (1) The marriage must be valid, and (2) both spouses must be baptized. A valid marriage may exist when one or both spouses are not baptized, but such a marriage is not sacramental. Prior to your wife's baptism, your marriage was presumably valid but not sacramental because she was not baptized. Her baptism did not in any way invalidate your marriage so, upon her baptism: (1) Your marriage remained valid, and (2) you both were baptized. Both of the requirements for a sacramental marriage being met, your marriage became sacramental at your wife's baptism.

The *Code of Canon Law* explains:

> The matrimonial covenant, by which a man and a woman establish between themselves a partnership of the whole of life and which is ordered by its nature to the good of the spouses and the procreation and education of offspring, has been raised by Christ the Lord to the dignity of a sacrament between the baptized. For this reason, a valid matrimonial contract cannot exist between the baptized without it being by that fact a sacrament. (CIC 1055)

Q: **My husband and I were married in the Catholic Church. My husband was a baptized Catholic, but I had not yet been baptized at the time. I have since been baptized. Is our marriage now sacramental?**

A: For marriage to be sacramental both spouses must be baptized. Prior to your baptism your marriage was presumably valid but not sacramental. When you became baptized your marriage automatically became sacramental.So what does this mean for your marriage? The *Catechism* explains:

> "By reason of their state in life and of their order, [Christian spouses] have their own special gifts in the people of God." This grace proper to the sacrament of matrimony is intended to perfect the couple's love and to strengthen their indissoluble unity. By this grace they "help one another to attain holiness in their married life and in welcoming and educating their children." (CCC 1641; cf. *Lumen Gentium* 11)

Q: I am a Methodist currently dating a girl who is Catholic. How does the Church feel about Catholics marrying non-Catholics, and what would we have to do? (Also, I am not very attached to the Methodist faith.)

A: Mixed marriages are discouraged because they inevitably involve pain for the spouses (the only time they don't is if neither spouse cares about his or her religion), and they set a bad example for the children because the parents are not united in the most important area of life—their relationship to God. This can lead to confusion, weak faith, and even lost faith on the part of the children.

Although mixed marriages are not recommended, the Church grants dispensations for Catholics to marry non-Catholics. To see about obtaining one you should see a parish priest.

If you are thinking seriously about marriage, I would urge you to investigate the Catholic faith and consider becoming a Catholic. It is far better on a human level if the spouses are religiously united. It is better both for children they have and for them, not only in that it prevents conflict but also in that it allows them to share true spiritual intimacy, which they otherwise are blocked from having.

Q: I am a Catholic who was married outside the Church without a dispensation, so my marriage is invalid—a fact I very much want to correct. My non-Catholic spouse is unwilling to be married in the Catholic Church. What can I do?

A: Assuming that there is nothing like a previous marriage that needs to be taken care of first (through a decree of nullity), and assuming that you both still have valid matrimonial consent, your marriage can be rendered valid using a procedure known as radical sanation.

This term comes from the Latin phrase *sanatio in radice*, meaning "healing in the root." According to the *Code of Canon Law*, "The radical sanation of an invalid marriage is its convalidation without the renewal of consent" (CIC 1161:1). This means you do not have to go through a new marriage ceremony.

For a radical sanation to take place, several conditions must apply. First, "A radical sanation is not to be granted unless it is probable that the parties intend to persevere in conjugal life" (CIC 1161:3).

Second, "A marriage cannot be radically sanated if consent is lacking in either or both of the parties" (CIC 1162:1).

Third, any impediments that exist must be taken care of.

Also, "A sanation can be granted validly even when one or both of the parties are unaware of it, but it is not to be granted except for serious reason" (CIC 1164).

Call your parish priest or your diocese to investigate obtaining a radical sanation.

Q: When a Catholic wishes to marry a non-Catholic, what is required by the Church?

A: The *Code of Canon Law* states:

> A marriage between two persons, one of whom has been baptized in the Catholic Church or received into it . . . and the other of whom is not baptized, is invalid (CIC 1086). A marriage is prohibited between two baptized persons of whom one is baptized in the Catholic Church or received into it after baptism . . . and the other of whom is enrolled in a church or ecclesial community not in full communion with the Catholic Church. (CIC 1124)

That said, the Church does sometimes allow such marriages under certain conditions:

- The Catholic party is to declare that he or she is prepared to remove dangers of defecting from the faith and is to make a sincere promise to do all in his or her power so that all offspring are baptized and brought up in the Catholic Church.
- The other party is to be informed at an appropriate time about the promises that the Catholic party is to make, in such a way that it is certain that he or she is truly aware of the promise and obligation of the Catholic party.
- Both parties are to be instructed about the purposes and essential properties of marriage, which neither of the contracting parties is to exclude. (CIC 1125 §1-3)

Q: When a Catholic and a non-Catholic get married, does the non-Catholic have to promise to raise the children of the marriage in the Catholic faith?

A: No. This used to be the case, but the current *Code of Canon Law* (1983) does not require the non-Catholic to make this promise. The *Code* does state that "the Catholic party . . . [must] promise to do all in his or her power to have all the children baptized and brought up in the Catholic Church" (1125), but the non-Catholic party does not have to promise to have the children raised Catholic.

This rule attempts to do justice to the consciences of both the Catholic and the non-Catholic. The non-Catholic party is not asked to violate his conscience if it requires him to refuse to promise to raise the children Catholic, and the Catholic party is asked to live out the belief that Catholicism is true by doing all that is possible to have the children raised in the truth. The final decision about how the children will be raised is to be a joint decision made by both parents. Canon law requires that all of this be understood by both parties before the marriage is contracted.

Q: My Protestant cousin is marrying a Catholic woman in a Catholic church, but he is not willing to raise any children they may have as Catholics. Can you explain how any priest would agree to celebrate this marriage?

A: In addition to the requirement that she "declare that [she] is prepared to remove dangers of defecting from the faith," the *Code of Canon Law* requires your cousin's bride-to-be to "make a sincere promise to do all in [her] power so that all offspring are baptized and brought up in the Catholic Church" (CIC 1125 §1). Your cousin, on the other hand, need only "be informed at an appropriate time about the promises which [she] is to make, in such a way that it is certain that [he] is truly aware of [her] promise and obligation" (CIC 1125 §2). He is not required to make the same promises. In fact, the marriage can go forward even if he is resistant to her promises.

Q: I am married to an ex-Catholic, now a non-Christian. I have been told that I should not have children if my husband refuses to raise them Catholic. Is this true?

A: You have been misinformed. The Church does not expect you to close yourself to the possibility of children simply because your husband is not Christian. The Church expects you to do the best that you can to raise your children Catholic. If your husband was Catholic at the time of your marriage, then he should respect the fact that the two of you went into marriage with the agreement that the children would be raised Catholic. If he was not Catholic at the time of the marriage, then you took a chance that he would allow you to raise the children Catholic and would not interfere in their Catholic education. This is one reason the Church strongly discourages interfaith marriages (while providing for their validity if the couple insists on marrying each other). Marriage includes the responsibility of being open to new life and open to building a family with your husband. You should not deny him the privilege of children of his own based on what you think he might do should they come along. Instead, you should sit down with him now, share your concerns, and seek to work out with him an agreement on how your children will be raised. If need be, a marital counselor can facilitate the discussion.

Q: Can I get my marriage to a non-Christian blessed by the Catholic Church?

A: If there are no other impediments to the marriage, you can—and indeed are obliged to—have your marriage convalidated by the Church. As a Catholic, you are under Church law and your marriage must be recognized by the Church in order to be valid. Once your marriage is convalidated, you will have a valid union (though not a sacramental one, since those who are not baptized cannot participate in the other sacraments). See your local priest about having your marriage convalidated. It should be a fairly simple thing to do.

Marriage

Q: When is marriage a sacrament?

A: The *Code of Canon Law* recognizes that, "a valid matrimonial contract cannot exist between the baptized without it being by that fact a sacrament" (CIC 1055 §2). So there are two requirements for a marriage to be a sacramental marriage: (1) the marriage must be valid; and (2) both parties must be baptized.

To be in a valid marriage, Catholics must meet certain requirements of canon law including the obligation to observe the Church's form of marriage celebration or to be dispensed from that form. This applies to every Catholic, even when marrying a non-Catholic.

All valid marriages between Catholics are sacramental because you can't be Catholic without being baptized. However, a valid marriage between a Catholic and a baptized non-Catholic is sacramental, while a valid marriage between a Catholic and a non-baptized person is not.

Non-Catholics are not generally under the authority of canon law concerning marriage, so marriages between non-Catholics are generally recognized to be valid unless proven otherwise. Some of these marriages are sacramental (when both parties are baptized) and some are not (when one or both are not baptized).

Q: Are non-Catholic marriages valid in the eyes of the Catholic Church?

A: In general, marriages between non-Catholics, of whatever religion, are considered valid, but the situation is not as simple as it sounds because there are two kinds of marriage: natural (ordinary) marriage and supernatural (sacramental) marriage. Supernatural marriages exist only between baptized people, so marriages between two Jews or two Muslims are only natural marriages. Assuming no impediments, marriages between Jews or Muslims would be valid natural marriages. Marriages between two Protestants or two Eastern Orthodox also would be valid, presuming no impediments, but these would be supernatural (sacramental) marriages and thus indissoluble.

Q: My godson is marrying outside the Church. I want to tell him why he must marry in the Church, but I don't know how much pressure to apply. My friends suggest I insist he marry in the Church. What do I do?

A: The Church teaches that:

> Only those marriages are valid which are contracted in the presence of the local ordinary or parish priest or of the priest or deacon delegated by either of them, who, in the presence of two witnesses, assists, in accordance however with the rules set out in the following canons. (CIC 1108 §1)

Of course you shouldn't try to force the couple to marry in the Church. But that doesn't mean that they shouldn't marry in the Church, or that you should not make your position known. It means only that the responsibility to marry in the Church is theirs and not yours.

I encourage you to inform your godchild of his obligation to marry in the Church. Perhaps you can offer him some reading materials on the importance of being validly married. If he refuses to listen to you, then at least you did your best.

Q: Can you explain why baptism outside the Church is valid but marriage outside the Church is not?

A: When administered outside the Church, both of these sacraments may be considered valid. But Church law obliges Catholics to wed in the Church or to obtain formal permission to wed outside it (CIC 1108). *The New Commentary on the Code of Canon Law* explains the reasons:

> At a pastoral level, the requirement of canonical form provides a privileged opportunity for the Church's ministers to help couples to assess their suitability and readiness for marriage and to provide them with the appropriate catechesis and immediate preparation for marriage and its liturgical celebration. At a more theological level, the mandatory form ensures that celebration of marriage will embody at least the minimal ecclesial and liturgical dimensions consistent with the celebration of a sacrament of the Church. (*New Commentary on the Code of Canon Law*, 1327)

Baptism is a different story. Jesus willed that everyone be baptized (Mt 28:19). Issues surrounding marriage (e.g., public character, one's suitability and readiness, appropriate catechesis, immediate preparation, minimal ecclesial and liturgical dimensions) are not applicable to baptism. Therefore, any baptism administered according to Jesus' instructions is valid.

Q: A priest told my girlfriend that it is okay for us to touch one another intimately before we are married. Is this correct?

A: No. Jesus stated in Matthew 5:28 that a person can commit sins of sexual impurity even in his thoughts. He stated, "But I say to you that everyone who looks at a woman lustfully has already committed adultery with her in his heart." The same thing is true of fornication (pre-marital sex).

Looking at a woman to whom you are not married and indulging in lustful thoughts counts as committing fornication in your heart. If indulging yourself in mental lust for a woman to whom you are not married counts, how much more will intimate touching, in which you partially act out the sexual desire you have for one another.

Though some priests may not like to say so, fornication is a grave (mortal) sin. The apostle Paul states, "Now the works of the flesh are plain: fornication, impurity, licentiousness . . . and the like. I warn you, as I warned you before, that those who do such things shall not inherit the kingdom of God" (Gal 5:19-21). This is a severe teaching. It is one many unmarried people find hard to accept, but it is the clear teaching of Scripture, and we must hold to it.

Q: I was told by a priest that sexual intercourse between unmarried persons is acceptable so long as it reflects a relationship of love. Lots of people seem to believe this, but is it true?

A: The only "relationship of love" that makes sexual intercourse acceptable is a marital one. The priest who told you otherwise wasn't presenting Catholic teaching on the subject, but his own (erroneous) opinion.

In its *Declaration on Certain Problems of Sexual Ethics*, the Vatican Congregation for the Doctrine of the Faith reaffirmed traditional Catholic teaching on the subject of sexual relations outside marriage:

> Nowadays many claim the right to sexual intercourse before marriage, at least for those who have a firm intention of marrying and whose love for one another, already conjugal as it were, is deemed to demand this as its natural outcome . . . This opinion is contrary to Christian teaching, which asserts that sexual intercourse may take place only within marriage. (7)

Q: If two people live together before marriage and do not go to confession before their wedding in a Catholic Church, is their marriage valid in the eyes of the Church?

A: The validity of the sacrament does not depend on the holiness of the couple.

> This is the meaning of the Church's affirmation that the sacraments act ex opere operato [literally, "by the very fact of the action being performed"], i.e., by virtue of the saving work of Christ, accomplished once for all. It follows that "the sacrament is not wrought by the righteousness of either the celebrant or the recipient but by the power of God." From the moment that a sacrament is celebrated in accordance with the intention of the Church, the power of Christ and his Spirit acts in and through it, independently of the personal holiness of the minister. (CCC 1128)

Q: **May two Baptists, baptized in the Trinity, married by a justice of the peace, and now going through RCIA to enter the Catholic Church, have their marriage convalidated immediately?**

A: From what you've stated, I don't see any reason that your marriage needs to be convalidated. Marriages between non-Catholics are generally considered valid unless proven otherwise. And since you both were apparently validly baptized (even though outside the Catholic Church), your marriage is also sacramental.

Q: Are sacraments efficacious even if not understood by the one receiving them? Doesn't grace require active cooperation of faith, knowledge, and will?

A: When a sacrament gives us a grace requiring cooperation, such as the grace to love our spouses, it does require us to cooperate for that grace to manifest itself. But when a sacrament gives us a grace that does not require action (such as sanctifying grace), then our active cooperation is not required. This is not to say that our passive cooperation is not needed. Sacraments communicate their grace to us unless we put obstacles in the way—but we can put obstacles in the way.

For example, in order to receive the sacrament of matrimony, it is necessary to be open to the essential properties of marriage, such as unity and indissolubility. If, at the time the marriage is contracted, one party is not open to the essential properties, the marriage will not be valid. There will be no real marriage at all.

The *Code of Canon Law* says, "But if either or both parties through a positive act of the will should exclude marriage itself, some essential element, or an essential property of marriage, it is invalidly contracted" (CIC 1102:2). But "error concerning the unity, indissolubility, or sacramental dignity of matrimony does not vitiate matrimonial consent so long as it does not determine the will" (CIC 1099).

Q: Is it possible for people of the same sex to marry each other?

A: No. Gay (or homosexual) "marriage" is not really marriage at all. Marriage was instituted by God as a relationship between a man and a woman. "Therefore a man leaves his father and his mother and cleaves to his wife, and they become one flesh" (Gn 2:24). The Church does not have the power or authority to change this—nor does secular society. Even if the legal definition of the word "marriage" were changed to include homosexual couples, those couples would not ever be truly married.

Q: Does the Bible say marriage is for a man and a woman?

A: Marriage between a man and a woman was instituted by God with Adam and Eve. Genesis 2:24 states: "Therefore a man leaves his father and his mother and cleaves to his wife, and they become one flesh."

In Matthew 19:4-5, we see Jesus reaffirming this: "Have you not read that he who made them from the beginning made them male and female, and said, 'For this reason a man shall leave his father and mother and be joined to his wife, and the two shall become one'?"

Q: I have a gay brother who has fallen from the faith. He has dated several guys over the last few years and wants to get "married" and adopt children in the future. I'm pretty certain that if I tell him I don't support him, it will ruin our relationship and create problems within the family. What should I do?

A: If you were attracted to a married woman and were in love with her, would you choose her over obeying the Lord or would you choose the Lord over her? It all boils down to how much we love him, doesn't it? He chose nothing over us. He willingly spent himself on us to the point of dying. This is the conversation you need to have with your brother. You both are in my prayers.

Q: I am a homosexual who wishes to obey the Church's teachings on homosexuality. I know that the Church teaches homosexual acts are wrong, but it teaches that all sex outside of marriage is wrong—a teaching which I support. What if two homosexuals were married to each other? Would sex between them be legitimate, and could the Church ever change its position and allow homosexuals to marry?

A: The answer to both questions is no. The reason homosexual acts are wrong is not simply that they take place outside of marriage, but that they are contrary to natural design. For various reasons, both inside and outside of their control, some people have desires that are not in accord with nature. When these desires are acted upon, the result is an unnatural and immoral act.

The Church cannot change its teaching on marriage, which is grounded in natural law. Under natural law a man can marry only whom he was designed to marry: a woman. He cannot validly marry another man any more than he could an animal or a plant. Any attempted marriage between a man and another man would be invalid by definition. It might be recognized by the state as a legitimate marriage, but it would not be so before God.

This is a difficult teaching to hear for one struggling with homosexual desires, but it is the truth. To get help, consider contacting Courage, a nationwide Catholic organization set up to help homosexuals lead chaste lives.

Q: We call Joseph Mary's "husband." I thought that if a marriage isn't consummated, it isn't technically a marriage. Is Joseph's title as Mary's husband merely honorary?

A: A man and a woman are truly married as soon as they commit themselves to each other by vow before God—not when the marriage is consummated. In a Christian context, a sacramental marriage becomes indissoluble when the marriage is consummated, but the marriage itself exists from the time the vows are said. Joseph and Mary were married under the Old Covenant and so their marriage wasn't the Christian sacrament, and wouldn't have been truly indissoluble in any case. But because they were pledged by oath to one another, their marriage was a true and valid one. Incidentally, the point is more than a technicality, since Matthew seems to predicate Jesus' messianic claim to the title "Son of David" (a phrase used throughout Matthew's Gospel) at least in part on his legal status as the son of Joseph, whom the angel addresses as "son of David" (Mt 1:20).

Q: Is it true that sexual intercourse between a married couple is sinful if the spouses do it with lust for each other?

A: I realize that in our culture the word "lust" can be understood quite broadly, from "lusting after a chocolate bar" to simply finding another person to be sexually attractive.

But for the Catholic Church, to lust is to seek sexual pleasure in another person solely for one's own pleasure without regard for the other person. The *Catechism of the Catholic Church* states: "Lust is disordered desire for or inordinate enjoyment of sexual pleasure. Sexual pleasure is morally disordered when sought for itself, isolated from its procreative and unitive purposes" (CCC 2351).

To have sexual feelings for one's spouse or to enjoy sexual pleasure with one's spouse is fine and according to God's design. But to use one's spouse as an object of pleasure without concern for the spouse is mortally sinful.

Q: Are marital relations not supposed to be pleasurable because they are only for reproductive purposes?

A: The primary purposes of marital relations are procreation and spousal unity (babies and bonding), but that does not mean that the husband and wife are not supposed to derive pleasure from their marital relations. Although pleasure is not a purpose of sex, it is important to fulfilling the purposes of sex.

God gave humans the capacity to enjoy food and sex in order to encourage them to fulfill the purposes of those human needs. A moral problem occurs only when deriving pleasure from food and sex is put above or in the place of its intended purpose. Someone who eats solely for pleasure, without regard for the needs of his body, abuses the privilege of eating. In the same way, someone who has sex solely for pleasure, without regard for its intended purposes of babies and bonding, abuses the privilege of sex.

Q: A friend said it doesn't make sense for the Church to permit Natural Family Planning (NFP) while banning the pill. Aren't these just two different ways of contracepting?

A: The mere fact that artificial contraception and NFP may have the same end in view doesn't mean they're morally equivalent. There's nothing wrong with avoiding pregnancy under certain circumstances. It's the means used to do so which are of concern here.

For example, you can support your family by honest work or you can rob banks. The end is the same, but the means used aren't morally equivalent. Honest labor is moral. Theft isn't.

NFP isn't contraception. In contraception an action is taken which prevents conception. In NFP, no such action occurs. Instead, sexual relations are avoided when conception is likely to occur.

Contraception violates the natural link between the procreative and unitive aspects of the marital act. This link, as *Humanae Vitae* teaches, is established by God and may not be broken by man on his own initiative (HV 12). NFP doesn't alter the marital act in any way.

Is it possible to misuse NFP? Yes. It can be used to exclude children from marriage altogether, for selfish, unchristian reasons, and that is counter to one of the purposes of marriage. In such an instance, the *purpose* for avoiding pregnancy is disordered, but not the means (NFP).

Q: Must I have a large family?

A: God said, "Be fruitful and multiply, and fill the earth . . ." (Gn 1:28). The *Catechism of the Catholic Church* teaches, "Sacred Scripture and the Church's traditional practice see in large families a sign of God's blessing and the parents' generosity" (2373).

Engendering and raising children is one of the primary purposes of marriage. The *Catechism* explains:

- The matrimonial covenant, by which a man and a woman establish between themselves a partnership of the whole of life, is by its nature ordered toward the good of the spouses and the procreation and education of offspring. (CCC 1601)

- Fecundity is a gift, an end of marriage, for conjugal love naturally tends to be fruitful. A child does not come from outside as something added on to the mutual love of the spouses, but springs from the very heart of that mutual giving, as its fruit and fulfillment. (CCC 2366)

That said, couples have a moral obligation to plan families responsibly:

- A particular aspect of this responsibility concerns the regulation of procreation. For just reasons, spouses may wish to space the births of their children. It is their duty to make certain that their desire is not motivated by selfishness but is in conformity with the generosity appropriate to responsible parenthood. (CCC 2368)

- Ultimately, family size should be determined by responsible procreation in cooperation with the love of God the Creator. (cf. CCC 2367)

Q: What is the official position of the Catholic Church with regard to in vitro fertilization (IVF)?

A: There is a whole mess of problems with IVF, and some techniques are worse than others. Some, for example, collect the germ cells from the wrong people (i.e., who are not married to each other) or collect them in a morally illicit manner. Some also produce large numbers of children who are either allowed to die or who are frozen indefinitely.

The least objectionable version would be homologous (married-couple) IVF where the germ cells are collected from married parents in a morally licit manner and everything is done to protect the life of the child or children thus conceived. However, even this form of IVF is immoral.

In its instruction *Donum Vitae*, the Congregation for the Doctrine of the Faith (CDF) explains that "the Church remains opposed from the moral point of view to homologous in vitro fertilization. Such fertilization is in itself illicit and in opposition to the dignity of procreation and of the conjugal union, even when everything is done to avoid the death of the human embryo."

The CDF also notes, "Although the manner in which human conception is achieved with IVF and ET [embryo transplant] cannot be approved, every child who comes into the world must in any case be accepted as a living gift of the divine goodness and must be brought up with love."

Q: I have a married friend who flirts. She sees nothing wrong with it, and says it doesn't lead to anything. I believe it's a sin. Is it?

A: It's not a sin if the individuals involved are not married. It's also not a sin if it is between people who are married to each other. But it is a sin if it is between a married person and someone other than her spouse, as in the case you mention. Your friend needs to get her act together. She owes such attention to her husband exclusively.

Q: My husband had an affair with a co-worker and got her pregnant. I am having a hard time forgiving and trusting him again. My priest told me to stop wallowing in self-pity and look at the pregnancy as a blessing.

A: The pregnancy is a blessing for the baby—but certainly not for you! Our crucified Savior is the solution. He knows what it is like to be betrayed and has given you an opportunity to share in his Passion in this way. Not only did Judas betray him, Peter denied him three times and the rest of the apostles abandoned him, leaving him quite alone before those who apprehended him. Have no doubt, Jesus is very aware of your plight and loves you. To have difficulty trusting a husband who betrayed you is not "wallowing in self-pity." It's a very normal reaction.

While the inanimate sign of the crucifix can help to direct your attention to the Savior's unlimited love for us, the Eucharist is the living sign of it. The sight of his blood separated from his body on the altar is enough to break your heart if you let the reality sink in. Such will be your consolation. There simply is none greater! Spend time each day going over his entire Passion in your mind and thanking him for each suffering. This will focus you and give you perspective. You will know his peace and the ability to forgive your husband—and the priest as well.

Q: A Mormon recently challenged me: Where in the Bible does it say that polygamy is wrong?

A: Be careful of falling into the trap of thinking that every point of faith and morals has to be explicitly attested in Scripture. That isn't the case.

Scripture indicates that for a time God did tolerate polygamy during the Old Testament. However, it was portrayed even then as a negative thing. When Scripture describes the domestic life of polygamists, it brings out consistently the negative effects of polygamy—jealousy, taunting, conflict, favoritism. (Take for example the strife between the wives of Abraham, Jacob, or Elkana; see Gn 21, 29-30, 1 Sm 1).

The problems were so clearly recognized that there had to be special legislation concerning polygamy. Thus a husband playing favorites was not allowed to deprive the children of his first wife their inheritance rights in favor of the children of a more recent wife (Dt 21:15-16). Kings were forbidden to multiply wives to themselves (Dt 17:17).

As time progressed, the problems with polygamy became more and more obvious, and it stopped being practiced.

Jesus indicated that marriage was to be restored to the state God had intended in Genesis 2. Thus Jesus prohibits divorce (Mk 10:2-9) on the grounds that it was not provided for in God's original plan. God made one man and one woman to be together. Polygamy is ruled out similarly.

Q: The Catholic Church forbids priests to marry. According to 1 Timothy 4:3, this is a "demonic doctrine," and therefore the Church is apostate.

A: Let's get this straight. The passage talks about false teachers who "forbid marriage." Does the Catholic Church do that? Not at all. If you would like to marry in the Catholic Church, you may do so by receiving the sacrament of holy matrimony (notice that it is regarded as holy and as a sacrament). Far from declaring marriages to be evil or forbidding them, the Church blesses them by giving a man and woman the opportunity to confer this holy sacrament on each other. What you are referring to is that, in the Latin rite of the Church, the clergy are not allowed to marry.

Apart from exceptional cases, married men are not allowed to be ordained. But no man is obliged to become a member of the clergy. Doing so is voluntary. True, a priest may not marry, but he agreed to that restriction before his ordinations (first to the diaconate and then to the presbyterate).

What 1 Timothy 4:3 is talking about are those sects that claim that marriage is evil, such as the Albigensians of the Middle Ages or the Shakers of more recent times.

Q: Why can't a priest marry?

A: The reasons Latin rite priests can't marry are both theological and canonical.

Theologically, priests serve in the place of Christ and therefore their ministry specially configures them to Christ. As is clear from Scripture, Christ was not married (except in a mystical sense, to the Church). By remaining celibate and devoting themselves to the service of the Church, priests more closely model, configure themselves to, and consecrate themselves to Christ.

As Christ himself makes clear, none of us will be married in heaven (Mt 22:23-30). By remaining unmarried in this life, priests are more closely configured to the final, eschatological state that will be all of ours.

Paul makes it very clear that remaining single allows a person's attention to be undivided in serving the Lord (1 Cor 7:32-35). He recommends celibacy to all (1 Cor 7:7) but especially to ministers, who as soldiers of Christ he urges to abstain from "civilian affairs" (2 Tm 2:3-4).

Canonically, priests cannot marry for a number of reasons. First, priests who belong to religious orders take vows of celibacy. Second, while diocesan priests do not take vows, they do make promises of celibacy. Third, the Church has established impediments that block the validity of marriages attempted by priests (CIC 1087).

A priest cannot be validly married after ordination unless he receives a dispensation from the Holy See (CIC 1078 §2, 1).

Q: Eastern-rite Catholics allow for the priestly ordination of married men. Since they are in communion with Rome, why are they not held to the same discipline as Roman-rite priests?

A: Because priestly celibacy is a discipline, not a doctrine, there is room for diversity on the issue according to the customs of the respective rites. If celibacy were a doctrine, all rites would have to conform to the judgment of the Holy See on the matter because doctrines are true for everybody. But celibacy is a discipline (a practice that is legislated by proper ecclesial authority) that has been deemed to be spiritually beneficial. In the Latin rite, this spiritual discipline ordinarily is required of all men who seek priestly ordination. In the Eastern rites, it is practiced by the monks and by some secular priests, but it is not required of all men who seek ordination. Out of respect for the longstanding customs of the Eastern-rite churches, the Vatican allows the Eastern churches in communion with the Holy See to maintain their own properly constituted discipline on this issue.

Q: In a non-Catholic marriage, if one spouse becomes Catholic and the other does not, can the spouse that joins the Church receive Communion? Is the couple living in sin?

A: Marriages between non-Catholics are considered to be valid unless something renders a particular one invalid. If one spouse later becomes Catholic this in no way invalidates the marriage. The couple would not be "living in sin," and the Catholic would be able to receive the Eucharist.

Divorce

Q: I'm thinking about divorce. What does the Catholic Church have to say about it?

A: Jesus said, "What therefore God has joined together, let not man put asunder" (Mk 10:9). So, although the Catholic Church recognizes the need for civil divorce in some circumstances, the Church also teaches that divorce does not dissolve the marriage bond before God. Therefore, even in situations where civil divorce is tolerated, divorce does not free the spouses to marry again. Cardinal William Levada, Prefect of the Congregation for the Doctrine of the Faith, explains:

> [Divorce is] the claim that the indissoluble marriage bond validly entered into between a man and a woman is broken. A civil dissolution of the marriage contract (divorce) does not free persons from a valid marriage before God; remarriage would not be morally licit.

If there are sufficient reasons for obtaining a civil divorce in your case, then it would be morally permissible to pursue one, but this would not result in the ability to remarry unless, for example, you pursued and received an annulment that showed your first marriage was invalid.

Q: A couple wants to have their marriage ended by the Church, and a priest said that they should ask about the Pauline Privilege. What is that, and how does it differ from an annulment?

A: A Pauline Privilege is the dissolution of a purely natural marriage which had been contracted between two non-Christians, one of whom has since become a Christian. The Pauline Privilege is so-named because it is based upon the apostle Paul's words in 1 Corinthians 7:12-16.

The Pauline Privilege differs from an annulment because it dissolves a real but natural marriage. An annulment is a declaration that there never was a valid marriage to begin with.The Pauline Privilege does not apply when two baptized people marry and later one quits being Christian. These people had a sacramental marriage forged between them and this marriage is indissoluble, even if one partner is failing to fulfill his marital responsibilities.

The Pauline Privilege also does not apply when a Christian has married a non-Christian. In those cases, a natural marriage exists and can be dissolved for a just cause, but by what is called the Petrine Privilege rather than by the Pauline Privilege. The Petrine Privilege is so-named because it is reserved to the Holy See, so only Rome can grant the Petrine Privilege (which it seldom does).

A biblical precedent for the Petrine Privilege, where some of the faithful marry unbelievers and then are permitted to divorce them, is found in Ezra 10:1-14.

Q: In Matthew 19:3-9, when the Pharisees are questioning Jesus about divorce, Jesus seems to make an exception in the case of adultery. Why, then, doesn't the Catholic Church follow what Jesus says in the Bible and allow divorce in such circumstances?

A: Let us recall first of all that Matthew's audience was mainly Jews, and only Matthew's Gospel has this exception clause.

The word "adultery" is not what Jesus said, although many Bible translations use this word. If Jesus intended to say adultery, he would have used the word *moicheia*, meaning "adultery," but instead he used the word *porneia*, meaning an illegal marriage.

His audience, the Jews, knew exactly what Jesus meant. Leviticus 18:6-16 lists marriages that are illegal for Jews because they are between certain degrees of consanguinity or are with a Gentile, which was forbidden. The Jews knew this, and this is why Matthew's Gospel includes this exception. The Catholic Church does follow what Jesus says, when his words are properly translated.

Q: My wife and I are considering divorce after a long and unloving period of our relationship. She considers us roommates. The reason we haven't divorced is that she couldn't live alone on her salary plus trying to raise our son. She is unwilling to go to counseling. What are the implications of divorce for practicing Catholics?

A: The one who loses here is your son. I would think long and hard before inflicting a divorce on him. You and your wife chose to marry each other. He didn't choose to be born. He deserves a home with a mother and a father. I'm not trying to lay a guilt trip on you. These are simply the facts. If it is absolutely impossible for the two of you to remain together, then the Church allows civil divorce for the equitable division of goods that have been held in common. I know of an instance where the child remained in the home and the parents would alternate every other week living there so that the child wouldn't be shuttled here and there for the rest of his childhood. I commend the parents for obviously being more concerned about him than about themselves. If you do divorce you are still married, and dating other people is out of the question unless and until you are able to have the marriage annulled.

Q: I am in the midst of a divorce I believe could be avoided with counseling, but my wife is moving toward the divorce with no second thoughts. Is it wrong for me to sign divorce papers? If I don't, she can still divorce me, but we would have to go through a trial, and that would ruin me financially.

A: Civil divorce has no effect on the indissolubility of a valid marriage. The Church permits civil divorce only for the equitable division of property that has been held in common. If not signing the divorce papers will not prevent the divorce, then refusing to do so might be only a waste of time and money. You are not obliged to incur financial ruin in order to avoid signing divorce papers.

Q: Is it a sin to divorce a spouse who is physically and emotionally abusive, after many attempts at resolving the behavior in couples therapy have failed?

A: No, it is not a sin to divorce such a spouse. The *Code of Canon Law* states:

> A spouse who occasions grave danger of soul or body to the other or to the children, or otherwise makes the common life unduly difficult, provides the other spouse with a reason to leave, either by a decree of the local ordinary [e.g., bishop] or, if there is danger in delay, even on his or her own authority. (CIC 1153)

The canon does go on to state that once such a danger has passed, common life should be restored, but given the unique difficulties of abuse cases (e.g., promises to reform are all too often broken), an abused spouse may wish to allow an independent specialist such as a priest or a psychologist to determine if and when it is safe to resume common life.

The Church considers civil divorce in such cases to be the ecclesial equivalent of a legal separation and tolerates civil divorce sought for just cause (such as to ensure personal safety or the safety of children) to settle estate and child custody arrangements. The divorced person is still considered validly married and may not remarry in the Church unless and until an annulment is granted.

Q: Can a divorced person without a Church annulment participate in the sacraments?

A: A divorced person is generally not required to seek an annulment unless he plans to attempt marriage again. And unless a person has been excommunicated (divorce is not cause for excommunication), a Catholic always has access to confession. In fact, a divorced Catholic should go to confession as soon as possible if the divorce was an occasion of mortal sin. If the divorce was not an occasion of mortal sin, then confession is not necessary. Either way, the Catholic would be able to lead a normal sacramental life.

Q: I'm divorced from my one marriage in the Catholic Church, but I never got an annulment. I was told since my marriage wasn't annulled that I could not receive the sacraments. Is that true?

A: Being divorced does not prevent you from receiving the sacraments. Neither does the fact that your prior marriage has not been annulled.

What would keep you from the sacraments is having attempted a new marriage without the former one being annulled. Any new marriage you may have attempted without an annulment will be presumed invalid, meaning that if you are living a conjugal life with a new partner you are presumed to be in a state of grave sin. It would be that sin, not being divorced without an annulment, that would keep you from receiving Communion.

If you have not attempted a new marriage since your previous one, or if you are living chastely until your current marital situation is rectified, then you can receive the sacraments.

Q: May a person who is divorced but not remarried receive Communion?

A: While Church teaching recognizes the seriousness of divorce, it understands that:

1. There are situations in which civil divorce may be necessary: "If civil divorce remains the only possible way of ensuring certain legal rights, the care of the children, or the protection of inheritance, it can be tolerated and does not constitute a moral offense" (CCC 2383), and

2. Divorce may occur due to no fault of an innocent spouse: "It can happen that one of the spouses is the innocent victim of a divorce decreed by civil law; this spouse therefore has not contravened the moral law. There is a considerable difference between a spouse who has sincerely tried to be faithful to the sacrament of marriage and is unjustly abandoned, and one who through his own grave fault destroys a canonically valid marriage." (CCC 2386)

In such cases, divorce is not sinful for that person and he or she may continue to receive Communion. However, in other cases—as with all serious sin—a divorced person should go to confession immediately, prior to receiving Communion.

Q: My brother was married outside the Church, then later he had the marriage blessed by a priest. He has since divorced and now he has stopped going to Mass. He tells me that there is no point in going to Mass if he can't go to Communion. What should I say?

A: The Sunday obligation for Catholics is a requirement to go to Mass, not to go to Communion (canon 1247). Naturally, every Catholic wants to go Communion at Mass, but the only obligation that applies is to attend Mass. Indeed, Catholics might have any number of reasons for not going to Communion: Perhaps they have not observed the one-hour fast or they feel they are in the state of grave sin and they need to go to confession first. But those factors do not affect the fact that all Catholics are obliged to attend Mass on Sunday in accord, of course, with the usual rules governing such obligations.

Moreover, the mere fact that your brother is divorced, even following his having the marriage "blessed" (technically, convalidated) in the Church, does not necessarily prevent him from going to Communion.

Q: Can divorced individuals become godparents or sponsors for baptism and confirmation?

A: If the person in question is living a life in keeping with the Church's expectations for someone in that situation, yes.

On the other hand, if the person does not have a Church annulment and is in a romantic relationship or has attempted remarriage outside the Church, then that person is not living "a life of faith that befits the role to be undertaken [i.e., baptismal or confirmation sponsor]," as required by canon law (CIC 874), and so another candidate for the role should be chosen.

Annulments

Q: For a while I could not receive Communion as a decision had not yet been made regarding the validity of my previous marriage. I have since wondered why the Church holds the worst sinners at arm's distance. Is the Eucharist truly the body and blood of Christ (who wants all sinners to come to him) or is it a "symbol" of our membership in this exclusive club called the Catholic Church?

A: The Church doesn't hold the worst sinners at arm's distance: The sinners themselves do. The Church isn't forcing them to sin. They are doing that quite on their own. The Church does not withhold the Lord's compassion any more than he did. But he was only compassionate with those who were repentant, and then he warned them not to engage in such activity again. When you were waiting for an annulment, you could have received Holy Communion if you were not having marital relations with someone with whom you were not validly married. Perhaps you didn't know that to do so is a grave sin. One cannot profess unconditional love for the Lord while at the same time engaging in sinful activity. The Church wasn't holding you at arm's distance. You could have gone to confession and determined to live as brother and sister until you were validly married—and then received Holy Communion. Many do. Unfortunately, priests often fail to tell people this.

Q: I have a friend who married outside the Church because there were problems with the annulment of a previous marriage. Why is she unable to receive Communion?

A: She chose to marry invalidly and live as though she were validly married—a grave situation. She will not be allowed to receive Communion as long as she ignores this. I recommend that she repent and go to confession, and that the couple commits to living as brother and sister until the situation is rectified (i.e., annulment and convalidation). Then she can receive Communion.

The *Catechism of the Catholic Church* explains:

> In fidelity to the words of Jesus Christ—"Whoever divorces his wife and marries another, commits adultery against her; and if she divorces her husband and marries another, she commits adultery" (Mk 10:11-12) —the Church maintains that a new union cannot be recognized as valid if the first marriage was. If the divorced are remarried civilly, they find themselves in a situation that objectively contravenes God's law. Consequently, they cannot receive eucharistic Communion as long as this situation persists. For the same reason, they cannot exercise certain ecclesial responsibilities. Reconciliation through the sacrament of penance can be granted only to those who have repented for having violated the sign of the covenant and of fidelity to Christ, and who are committed to living in complete continence. (CCC 1650)

Q: In the last couple years I have come back to the Church. I just went to confession, but the priest would not absolve me of my sins because I am still living in a non-sacramental marriage and my wife is agnostic. I asked him if it mattered that we are not having sexual relations. He said no and that I should encourage my wife to marry me in the Church. What should I do?

A: The priest gave you incorrect advice. So long as you are living a chaste lifestyle, you are entitled to receive absolution and then Holy Communion. You need to find another confessor. I would suggest that you receive Communion where your situation is not known so as not to give scandal to anyone who might not understand.

Q: I am a divorced Methodist who has been attending my local Catholic church. I would like to take the next step and become Catholic. Am I able to be confirmed, since I am divorced, or do I need to be granted an annulment first?

A: Divorce, in itself, is not an obstacle to confirmation. Sometimes, however, divorce is gravely sinful and unforgiven grave sin is something that needs to be taken care of by confession prior to confirmation. Annulments are generally only necessary if one wishes to attempt marriage again. It would not be necessary prior to reception into the Church unless you have attempted marriage after your divorce and wish to continue a conjugal life.

Q: My husband and I married in the Catholic Church, but now I am separated from him and in the process of divorce and annulment. Priests have told me that I can date and still receive the sacraments if the relationships are pure and entered into prayerfully. Is this correct?

A: No. Currently you are not even legally divorced, much less have you received a decree of nullity from the Church. Until the latter happens, you must presume that you are a married woman and may not date anyone. Once you are legally divorced, you will no longer be married in the eyes of the state, but you will be married in the eyes of the Church unless and until you receive an annulment—and there is never any guarantee that an annulment will be granted. If you maintain a life of chastity appropriate to your state as a married woman legally separated from her husband (the Church considers civil divorce the equivalent of a legal separation), and otherwise remain in a state of grace, you may receive the sacraments. Once an annulment is granted, then you will be free to date.

Q: A husband and wife are validly married in the Catholic Church, and after several years get a civil divorce, never seek an annulment, live chastely after the divorce, and then reconcile. Are they allowed to have intercourse since they are still married in the eyes of the Church, or must they first have their marriage acknowledged by the state?

A: For a Catholic, divorce is a purely civil matter and does not affect the validity of a sacramental marriage whatsoever. The husband and wife will always retain the right to express their marriage vows sexually. When such individuals reconcile, they are certainly free to live as man and wife.

Q: I am a cradle Catholic and was married in the Catholic Church 29 years ago. My husband had no faith background. After many years of disharmony and pain in our marriage, my husband converted to Catholicism. Now, after living our faith and marriage as it should have been all those years, we feel we truly understand the meaning and sacredness of our vows. Is there any spiritual benefit to renewing wedding vows, or is the ceremony merely symbolic? I have heard differing opinions from priests. I know we were truly married 29 years ago despite all the difficulties, but now we would express these vows more deeply, fully respecting and honoring this most holy sacrament.

A: The renewal of marriage vows is symbolic. If a marriage is valid, it can't be made more valid. However, renewing marriage vows can be a very effective reminder to the couple and all those present of the significance of the sacrament and how the power of God has brought the couple to such a milestone.

Q: If two Lutherans are married and they get a divorce in a civil court, can either remarry a Catholic in the Catholic Church?

A: If the prior marriage was a valid, sacramental marriage then only the death of one of the spouses frees the other to marry again. The Catholic Church is consistent with Jesus' teaching on this (see Mk 10:9).

Therefore, if one of the spouses wishes to remarry in the Catholic Church while the other spouse is still living, the prior marriage must first be investigated to determine whether it was valid and sacramental. If it was, a new marriage cannot take place. If it was not, the Church will declare this officially with a declaration of nullity and the party should be free to marry a Catholic in the Church if the Catholic receives the appropriate dispensation to marry a non-Catholic.

Q: How do I deal with legalism when I encounter it? Does God draw a distinction between somebody who marries carelessly and then goes through a Church annulment and somebody who gets a civil divorce then remarries?

A: Church annulment is the process by which it is determined that a valid marriage has not taken place, leaving the persons free to marry. Unless such proof can be obtained, a marriage is ordinarily presumed to be valid. One cannot be married to two people. A civil divorce has no power to dissolve a valid marriage. This is not an example of legalism. It is reasonable if one understands it.

Q: When a Protestant man and woman are married in a non-Catholic ceremony which is not celebrated by a Catholic priest, why does an annulment have to be obtained in the event one becomes Catholic and wants to remarry?

A: A consummated sacramental marriage is indissoluble by any human power. Jesus said, "What therefore God has joined together, let not man put asunder" (Mk 10:9). The Catholic Church takes this seriously and therefore will not take part in a new marriage when it believes another valid marriage may already exist. This is true even if that marriage is between Protestants married outside the Catholic Church—such marriages are recognized as valid by the Church.

Civil divorce is often man's attempt to put asunder what God has joined together, and the Church knows that man does not have the power or authority to do this. The annulment process is simply the Church's investigation into what looks like a marriage to determine whether a valid marriage really exists. If it does, the Church will not, indeed cannot, recognize another marriage. If, on the other hand, the Church finds that a valid marriage does not exist, then a new marriage, truly a first marriage (unless a valid previous marriage ended through death), may be celebrated.

Q: If it is determined by the proper tribunal that a valid marriage never existed, what exactly is an annulment "nullifying"?

A: An annulment is more accurately termed a "declaration of matrimonial nullity" and does not actually nullify anything. Rather, the annulment process determines whether what may appear to be a valid marriage is actually a valid marriage or not. If it is determined that a valid marriage does not exist, then it is declared that the marriage is null—that a valid marriage never existed.

In his book *Annulments and the Catholic Church*, Edward Peters explains that an annulment is:

> A juridic determination that, at the time of the wedding, one or both parties to the marriage lacked sufficient capacity for marriage, and/or that one or both parties failed to give adequately their consent to marriage as the Church understands and proclaims it, and/or, in weddings involving at least one Catholic, that the parties violated the Church's requirements of canonical form in getting married. (1-2)

Q: Divorce, if I understand correctly, is considered gravely sinful. Why then would the Church require divorce before consideration of an appeal for annulment? Isn't this choosing evil so that a greater good may come from it?

A: The Church does not officially require a civil divorce before accepting an annulment petition. But canon lawyer Edward Peters explains that virtually every tribunal in America requires proof of civil divorce because "many tribunals apparently fear that they can be sued by irate spouses for 'alienation of affection.'" Peters thinks this reason is "quite unsatisfying," but he holds that "a civil divorce is a practical way of determining that there is no realistic hope of reconciling the parties, something tribunal judges are required to verify as part of every tribunal case" (Peters, *Annulments and the Catholic Church*, 50). Note also that the *Catechism* states, "If civil divorce remains the only possible way of ensuring certain legal rights, the care of the children, or the protection of inheritance, it can be tolerated and does not constitute a moral offense" (CCC 2383).

Q: How can a couple live together for years and then have their marriage annulled?

A: This question proceeds from an assumption that the length of time a couple spends together makes it married. It doesn't. The state may have a provision for "common law marriages" under which a couple which lives together long enough becomes regarded by the state as married or pseudo-married, but God does not. If a couple lives together for years without getting married in God's eyes, the are still unmarried in God's eyes.

This is the principle which allows an annulment after a period of years. If a couple were never sacramentally married in God's eyes, the mere passage of time does not create the sacrament between them. Thus, if it can be established that their initial contracting of the marriage was invalid (due to an impediment or the fact that the couple did not exchange valid matrimonial consent), then, no matter how much time has elapsed, the two are not married because there never was a marriage in the first place.

A marriage must be valid before God from the time it was contracted, or it is not valid at all and thus can be annulled: that is, determined to have been invalid from the beginning.

Q: Why is a fee required for an annulment?

A: The fee helps cover the costs associated with processing the case, including the salaries of the experts who are kept on staff to examine such cases. In his book *Annulments and the Catholic Church*, canon lawyer Edward Peters states:

> First and most commonly, there are the basic petition fees payable to the tribunal. This is what most people refer to when they talk about the cost of an annulment. In the U.S. most tribunals charge anywhere from $200 to $1,000 for adjudicating a standard nullity case . . . These fees are typically payable over time, and there are means for having fees reduced or eliminated in cases of financial hardship (canon 1464). (7-8)

Q: **A member of a tribunal told me that a valid, consummated, sacramental marriage can be annulled on the basis of "incompatability of faith" even though *Handbook of Prayers* (Scepter Publishers, 1995), published by the authority of the NCCB, states: "The Church does not have the power to dissolve a valid sacramental marriage that has been consummated" (23). What can you tell me?**

A: The *Handbook of Prayers* is correct. The Church's Code of Canon Law agrees: "A marriage that is *ratum et consummatum* [meaning valid, sacramental, and consummated] can be dissolved by no human power and by no cause, except death" (CIC 1141).

I suspect that you misunderstood the tribunal member. To say that a valid marriage can be annulled makes no sense. An annulment never invalidates a marriage—it simply recognizes and declares that a valid marriage never existed. There are cases, however, in which a valid marriage that is either (1) not sacramental or (2) not consummated may be dissolved, but dissolution is very different from annulment in that dissolution actually ends marriage.

Q: Two people stated that the non-consummation of a marriage is grounds for a declaration of nullity—that is, an annulment. Surely this is incorrect, isn't it?

A: You are quite correct, at least as you have stated the issue. A decree of nullity indicates that a marriage was never valid from the beginning. Since consummation is not required for a marriage to be valid, non-consummation is not itself a ground for judging a marriage invalid from the beginning. That said, there are two caveats that need to be made.

First, if the marriage remains unconsummated for an unusual period of time, it may be due to something that did render the marriage invalid from the beginning (such as antecedent and perpetual impotence, *Code of Canon Law* 1084 §1). In this case, the non-consummation is not the grounds for nullity, it is an indicator that there may be some other condition that might be grounds.

Second, while non-consummation does not mean a null marriage, it does mean it is dissoluble. It is consummation that achieves the "one flesh" union (1 Cor 6:16) which Jesus says makes marriage indissoluble (Mk 10:7-9). Consequently, a decree of dissolution can be granted for a non-consummated marriage.

Q: If a couple is on contraception on their wedding day and are using it for years, could that be grounds for an annulment?

A: Use of contraception from the beginning of a marriage is not in and of itself grounds for finding the marriage to be null. But if from the outset either party has the explicit or implicit intention never to bring children into the world at all, or to deny the other's right to sexual acts open to procreation, this could make it possible to declare the marriage null and void.

Q: A young woman was coerced into marriage before being allowed to return to the U.S. from a foreign country. Once back in the U.S., she never lived with her husband. Might this be grounds for an annulment?

A: Yes, it sounds as though this marriage is not valid due to the coercion you describe. The *Code of Canon Law* states:

> No marriage can exist between a man and a woman who has been abducted or at least detained with a view of contracting marriage with her unless the woman chooses marriage of her own accord after she has been separated from the captor and established in a safe and free place. (CIC 1089)

Also, "[a] marriage is invalid if entered into because of force or grave fear from without, even if unintentionally inflicted, so that a person is compelled to choose marriage in order to be free from it" (CIC 1103).

Q: I'm thinking about obtaining an annulment from my previous marriage. My current marriage was before a justice of the peace. My husband and I would like to be married in the Catholic Church. My husband is a Presbyterian and I am Catholic. Does he have to become a Catholic in order to be married in the Catholic Church? Will he also have to have his previous marriage annulled before he is married in the Catholic Church?

A: It will be necessary for both of your previous marriages to be declared null before you can have your current marriage blessed (convalidated) in the Church. Permission is required for a Catholic to marry a non-Catholic, but there is no requirement for the non-Catholic party to become Catholic.

The *Catechism* speaks to couples in a situation such as yours and encourages you to seek forgiveness and live chastely:

> If the divorced are remarried civilly, they find themselves in a situation that objectively contravenes God's law. Consequently, they cannot receive eucharistic Communion as long as this situation persists. . . . Reconciliation through the sacrament of penance can be granted only to those who have repented for having violated the sign of the covenant and of fidelity to Christ and who are committed to living in complete continence. (CCC 1650)

Q: My first wife and I were married by the justice of the peace. I was baptized in a Baptist church, but she was not baptized at all. Do I have to go through an annulment process?

A: Since neither you nor your wife was Catholic when you got married, there were no special permissions or dispensations required of either of you. The Church, therefore, presumes your marriage to be valid. If you wish to attempt marriage again, you will first need to have your marriage investigated for nullity (i.e., get an annulment) to be certain that it was invalid. If it was, then you should be free to attempt marriage again.

Q: I am a sponsor for a candidate for confirmation with RCIA. My candidate has a former husband who is a Protestant and is refusing to go through the annulment process. Does this mean that she cannot obtain an annulment?

A: No. Either party can petition for an annulment. Canon 1510 specifically provides for a respondent who refuses to accept a legitimately served citation, and Canon 1592 §1 allows the judge (tribunal) "to declare the respondent absent from the trial and decree that the case is to proceed to the definitive sentence and its execution." You might ask the candidate to pick up a copy of Edward N. Peters' book, *Annulments and the Catholic Church: Straight Answers to Tough Questions.*

Q: I was granted an annulment, and I've begun to wonder: Was I living in sin with my "spouse" during those years? Are our children considered illegitimate?

A: If by "living in sin" you mean fornication—a mortal sin—the answer is no. One requirement of mortal sin is full knowledge of the sin being committed. In a situation where the spouses are unaware of the invalidity of their union—what the Church calls a "putative marriage"—there is no sin of fornication, because this condition is not met.

The Church teaches that children born of a putative marriage (which exists when at least one spouse is convinced of the validity of a marriage and lasts until both are convinced of its invalidity) are considered legitimate, even if the marriage is later declared null (CIC 1137).

Illegitimacy is not a moral or spiritual state. It has no bearing on a child's soul or salvation. Historically, legitimacy impinged only upon canonical matters, being required for ordination or appointment as a prelate or abbot.

Q: My mother was divorced six years ago and has recently been thinking about starting the annulment process. Would my siblings and I be considered illegitimate, that since the marriage was annulled it is considered to never have existed, thus making us born out of wedlock?

A: The bottom line answer to your question is that an annulment has no effect whatsoever on the legitimacy or illegitimacy of the children born from a particular union. Children either are or are not illegitimate, regardless of whether an annulment is granted or not.

Most of the time, even when an annulment is granted, the children are still legitimate. This is because canon law specifies that "Children conceived or born of a valid or putative marriage are legitimate" (CIC 1137). "An invalid marriage is called putative if it has been celebrated in good faith by at least one of the parties, until both parties become certain of its nullity" (CIC 1061 §3). This means that as long as one of the parties thought they were married, all of the children born of that union will be legitimate.

It is also possible, even when children have been born illegitimately that they can be rendered canonically legitimate (CIC 1139). This is possible because legitimacy is a legal rather than a moral concept. It is used in various law systems to determine such things as child support and inheritance rights, but it is no reflection on the child.

Q: Can you become engaged while waiting for an annulment?

A: Moral law would indicate that, apart from exceptional circumstances, the answer is no. A declaration of nullity—commonly called an annulment—establishes that one is free to marry. Since marriage enjoys the favor of the law, until the annulment is granted, the presumption is that a person will not be able to marry. He should act in accordance with that presumption until the contrary is established.

Failure to do so can lead to dire consequences. If you get engaged prior to receiving a declaration of nullity and it turns out that one is not granted, then you will be in a very difficult situation. You will have gotten your hopes up for a situation that cannot come to pass. You will have done the same thing to another person—your fiancée or fiancé—whom you profess to love. Real love would not put another individual in such a position. Finally, many Catholics in your situation would find themselves in a near occasion of mortal sin, as they would be tempted to "jump ship" and have a wedding outside the Church. This, of course, would result in an invalid union and a state of living in grave sin.

All told, it is far more responsible to act in accordance with the presumption that you are not free to marry until it is shown that you are. It spares everyone a world of hurt and temptation.

Q: I was married in the Church, later divorced, and then I remarried. I just received word that my annulment request was denied. However, my deacon told me that if I believe in good conscience that my first marriage was not valid, I can return to the Eucharist. Is this true?

A: A Catholic cannot use his or her conscience (the internal forum) to overturn a ruling of the diocesan tribunal (external forum). Canon 1671 clearly states that "marriage cases of the baptized belong to the ecclesiastical judge by proper right." This is because "marriage is not simply a private decision," but a public one, involving the Church and the spouses, "both individually and as a couple." According to the Congregation for the Doctrine of the Faith's 1994 *Letter to the Bishops Concerning the Reception of Holy Communion by the Divorced and Remarried*, not to recognize the Church's mediation in the judgment of the nullity of a previous marriage, "would mean in fact to deny that marriage is a reality of the Church, that is to say, a sacrament" (8). Also:

> The mistaken conviction of a divorced and remarried person that he may receive Holy Communion normally presupposes that personal conscience is considered in the final analysis to be able, on the basis of one's own convictions, to come to a decision about the existence or absence of a previous marriage and the value of the new union. However, such a position is inadmissible. (7)

Q: Two of my friends are baptized Protestants and both were previously married to other Protestants before getting divorces and marrying each other. They have applied for annulments of their earlier marriages. Assuming both annulment petitions are granted, will they need to have their marriage to each other blessed in the Church?

A: No. As soon as both annulment petitions are formally granted, your friends' marriage to each other will automatically be recognized by the Church.

Here's why: At the time your friends married each other, the only canonical obstacle to their wedding was ligamen, the fact of their prior marriage bonds (canon 1085). But if annulments are declared for both prior marriages, that means that at the time of their marriage to each other your friends were canonically free to contract marriage and the manner in which they chose to marry would have been lawful for them at the time. Thus, their second marriage could be recognized without any further qualifications.

Q: Our sister's marriage recently was declared null. How should we react to that news?

A: First, a declaration of nullity is not a "victory" in the case of those who wanted it or as a "defeat" for those opposed. The Church doesn't look at it that way.

Neither is it a second chance to do something right; it is a recognition that the first time never satisfied the objective requirements of law. There is nothing satisfying about declaring marriages null. Every annulment, correctly decided, discloses a failure. It documents the frustration of one, and often two, people who tried to do what they thought was right and who might well have wanted to enter the kind of lifelong union the Church calls marriage. But for reasons centered in one or both parties, that attempt was null from the outset.

In annulment cases involving Catholics, every declaration of nullity represents the failure to identify factors which could threaten the validity of a marriage and address them adequately in advance, as called for in canon 1066. Every annulment is another voice calling for higher standards in marriage preparation programs, not lower.

Q: I've been told that a woman who was married, had children, and then got an annulment became a nun later in life. Is this possible?

A: Yes. And the same thing can happen with men becoming monks. It also sometimes happens that a religious order will accept an individual who is widowed rather than divorced. Such cases tend to happen only after the children are grown, since there is a grave moral obligation for parents to see to the support and education of their children. This makes such cases uncommon, since religious orders normally do not accept new members who are above a certain age. However, it is possible.

INDEX

Note: Numbers refer to question number.